Flower Fun

EASY

Size

About 46 inches square

Materials

Medium (worsted) weight yarn, 25 oz (7500 yds, 750g) white; 10 oz (600 yds, 300g) lime; 5 oz (300 yds, 150g) each turquoise, pink, orange and yellow

Size K/10½/6.5mm crochet hook or size needed to obtain gauge

Tapestry needle

Gauge

Square = 6½ inches square

Instructions

Turquoise Flower Square (make 13)

With lime, ch 9; join to form ring.

Rnd 1 (RS): Ch 3 (counts as dc on this and following rnds), 2 dc in ring; ch 6, sl st in side of last dc made; *3 dc in ring, ch 6, sl st in side of last dc made; rep from * 6 times, join in 3rd ch of beg ch-3. *(8 ch-6 sps)* Change to turquoise by drawing lp through; cut lime.

Rnd 2: Sl st in next dc; *12 dc in next ch-6 sp—petal made; sl st in 2nd dc of next 3-dc group; rep from * 6 times more; 12 dc in next ch-6 sp—petal made; join in first sl st. *(8 petals)* Change to white by drawing lp through; cut turquoise.

Rnd 3: Ch 1, sc in same sl st, ch 5, working behind petals made on previous rnd, sc in next sl st, ch 3; *sc in next sl st, ch 5, sc in next sl st, ch 3; rep from * twice more; join in first sc.

Rnd 4: Sl st in next ch-5 sp, ch 3, in same sp work (2 dc, ch 3, 3 dc)—beg corner made; 3 dc in next ch-3 sp; *in next ch-5 sp work (3 dc, ch 3, 3 dc)—corner made; 3 dc in next ch-3 sp; rep from * twice more; join in 3rd ch of beg ch-3.

Rnd 5: Ch 4 (counts as a dc and a ch-1 sp), sk next dc, dc in next dc, ch 1; *in next corner ch-3 sp work (dc, ch 3, dc)—corner made; ch 1, [dc in next dc, sk next dc, ch 1] 5 times; rep from * twice more; in next corner ch-3 sp work (dc, ch 3, dc)—corner made; ch 1, [dc in next dc, sk next dc, ch 1] 3 times; join in 3rd ch of beg ch-4.

Rnd 6: Ch 3, [dc in next ch-1 sp and in next dc] twice; *in next corner ch-3 sp work (dc, ch 3, dc)—corner made; dc in each ch-1 sp and in each dc to next corner ch-3 sp; rep from * twice more; in next corner ch-3 sp work (dc, ch 3, dc)—corner made; dc in each ch-1 sp and in each dc to beg ch-3; join in 3rd ch of beg ch-3.

Rnd 7: Ch 1; *sc in each dc to next corner ch-3 sp; 5 sc in corner ch-3 sp; rep from * twice more; sc in each dc to first sc; join in first sc.

Fasten off and weave in all ends.

Pink Flower Square (make 12)

Work same as Turquoise Flower Square, changing to pink at end of rnd 1.

Yellow Flower Square (make 12)

Work same as Turquoise Flower Square, changing to yellow at end of rnd 1.

Orange Flower Square (make 12)

Work same as Turquoise Flower Square, changing to orange at end of rnd 1.

Assembly

Referring to diagram for color placement, join squares tog. To join squares, hold 2 squares with right sides tog and carefully match sts. With white and beg and ending in 3rd sc of each corner, sc through back lps only of each sc. Join rem squares in same manner, making sure all 4-corner junctions are securely joined.

Border

Hold afghan with RS facing you and one end at top; join lime in 3rd sc of upper right-hand corner.

Rnd 1: Ch 1, 3 sc in same sc—corner made; *sc in each sc to 3rd sc of next corner; 3 sc in 3rd sc—corner made; rep from * twice more; sc in each sc to first sc; join in first sc.

Rnd 2: Ch 1, sc in same sc; 3 sc in next sc—corner made; sc in each sc to 2nd sc of next corner; 3 sc in 2nd sc—corner made; rep from * twice more; sc in each sc to first sc; join in first sc.

Fasten off and weave in ends.

COLOR KEY
Y=Yellow flower square
P=Pink flower square
T=Turquoise flower square
O=Orange flower square

Y	P	T	O	T	P	Y
P	T	O	Y	O	T	P
T	O	Y	P	Y	O	T
O	Y	P	T	P	Y	O
T	O	Y	P	Y	O	T
P	T	O	Y	O	T	P
Y	P	T	O	T	P	Y

Flower Fun Afghan

Lofty Throw

EASY

Size

About 40 x 60 inches without fringe

Materials

Super bulky (bulky) weight yarn, 36 oz (855 yds, 1017g) variegated; 6 oz (100 yds, 170g) lime

Note: *Our photographed afghan was made with Coats & Clark Red Heart Bright and Lofty, beach #9955; Red Heart Grande, lime #2652.*

Size N/15/10mm crochet hook or size needed to obtain gauge

Tapestry needle

Gauge

6 hdc = 4 inches

Instructions

With variegated, ch 60.

Row 1 (RS): Hdc in 3rd ch from hook (beg 2 skipped chs count as a hdc) and in each rem ch, turn. *(59 hdc)*

Row 2: Ch 2 (counts as a hdc on this and following rows); ***hdc in next hdc, sk next hdc, ch 1; rep from * to last hdc and beg 2 skipped chs; hdc in last hdc and in 2nd ch of beg 2 skipped chs, turn.

Row 3: Ch 2, hdc in each hdc, in each ch-1 sp and in 2nd ch of turning ch-2, turn.

Row 4: Ch 2, hdc in each hdc and in 2nd ch of turning ch-2, turn.

Rep row 4 until piece measures about 58 inches.

Next Row: Ch 2; ***hdc in next hdc, sk next hdc, ch 1; rep from * to last hdc and turning ch-2; hdc in last hdc and in 2nd ch of turning ch-2, turn.

Last Row: Ch 2, hdc in each hdc, in each ch-1 sp and in 2nd ch of turning ch-2.

Fasten off and weave in all ends.

Fringe

Following Fringe instructions on page 14, make Double Knot Fringe. Cut 22-inch strands of lime; use 3 strands for each knot. Tie knot in each ch-1 sp across each short end of afghan. Trim ends evenly.

Reversible Stripes

EASY

Size
About 42 x 62 inches without fringe

Materials
Medium (worsted) weight yarn, 40 oz (1920 yds, 1128g) white

Light (sport) weight yarn, 7 oz (500 yds, 200g) each orange, red, green, yellow and blue

Note: *Our photographed afghan was made with Coats & Clark TLC Lustre, white #5001; TLC Wiggles, orange #209, cherry #423, green #727, yellow #158 and blue #608.*

Size I/9/5.5mm crochet hook or size required to obtain gauge

Tapestry needle

Gauge
In pattern, 11 sts = 4 inches

Instructions
Note: *At beg and end of each row, leave a 9-inch end to be included in fringe.*

With white, ch 170.

Row 1 (RS): Sc in 2nd ch from hook and in each rem ch. *(169 sc)* Fasten off *(see Note).*

Row 2: Hold piece with WS facing you; join orange in first sc, ch 3 (counts as dc on this and following rows), dc in each rem sc. Fasten off.

Row 3: Hold piece with RS facing you; join white in first dc; ch 1, sc in same dc and in next dc; *tr in next sc (already worked) on row 1; on working row, sc in next dc; rep from * to beg ch-3; sc in 3rd ch of beg ch-3. Fasten off.

Row 4: Hold piece with WS facing you; join red in first sc, ch 3, dc in each rem sc. Fasten off.

Row 5: Hold piece with RS facing you; join white in first dc; ch 1, sc in same dc and in next dc; *tr in next sc (already worked) on row below; on working row, sc in next dc; rep from * to beg ch-3; sc in 3rd ch of beg ch-3. Fasten off.

Row 6: With green, rep row 4.

Row 7: Rep row 5.

Row 8: With yellow, rep row 4.

Row 9: Rep row 5.

Row 10: With blue, rep row 4.

Row 11: Rep row 5.

Row 12: With orange, rep row 4.

Row 13: Rep row 5.

Rows 14–123: Rep rows 4 through 13 eleven times more.

Rows 124–127: Rep rows 4 through 7. At end of row 127, do not fasten off. Turn.

Row 128: Ch 1, sc in each st.

Fasten off.

Fringe
Following Fringe instructions on page 14, make Single Knot Fringe. Cut 14-inch strands of white; use 2 strands for each knot plus 2 ends (1 white and 1 contrasting color) left at edge of each white row. Tie knot in end of each white row across each short end of afghan. Trim ends evenly.

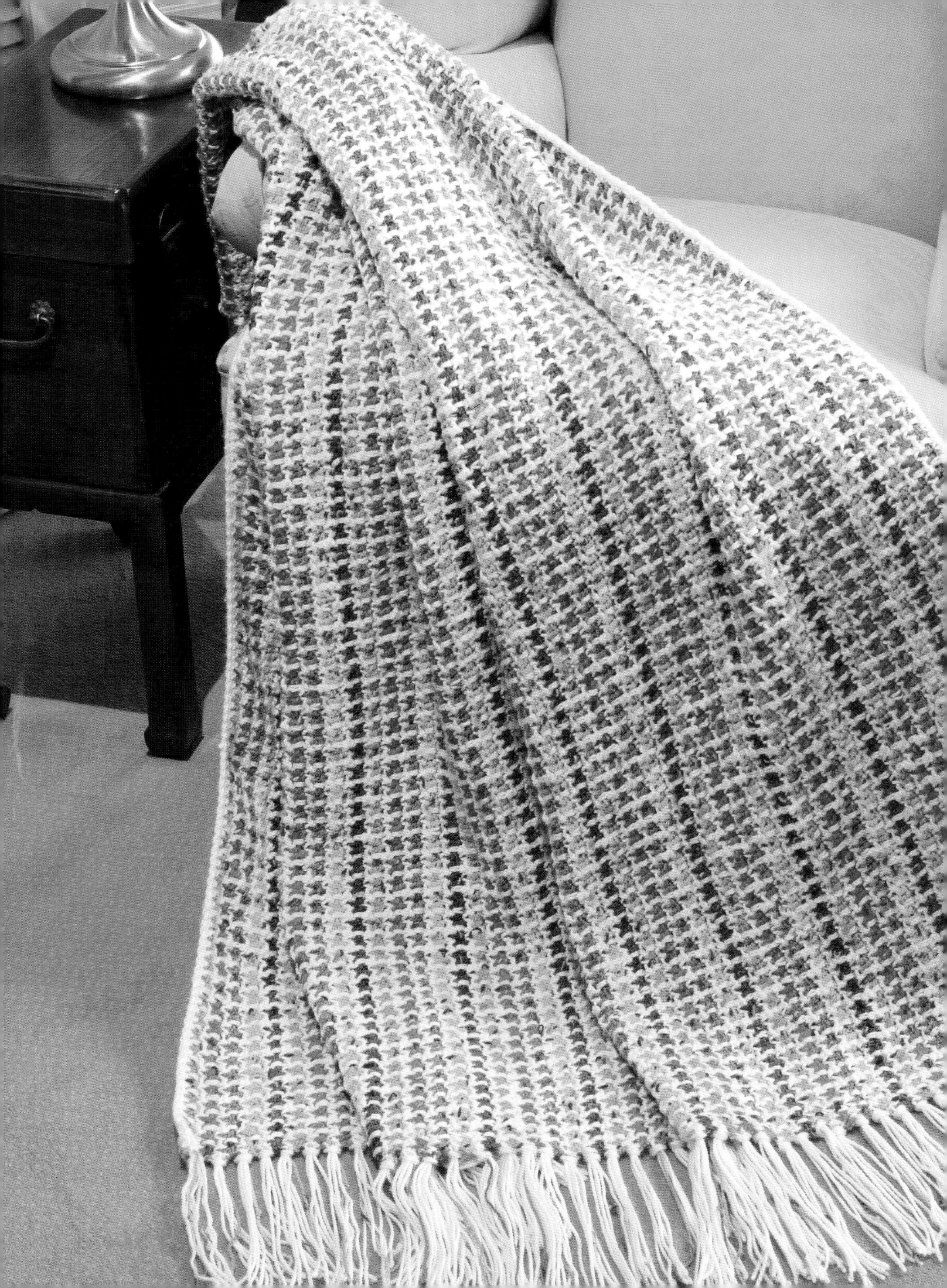

Ripples of Fun

EASY

Size

About 48 x 60 inches

Materials

Bulky (chunky) weight yarn, 37½ oz (855 yds, 1050g) variegated; 12 oz (465 yds, 339g) purple; 8 oz (310 yds, 226g) each light purple and yellow

Note: *Our photographed afghan was made with Lion Boucle, sprinkles #201; Lion Brand Chunky USA, napa grape #147, lavender jazz #143 and yukon gold #158.*

Size N/13/9mm crochet hook or size needed to obtain gauge

Tapestry needle

Gauge

In ripple pattern, 10 sts = 4 inches

Pattern Stitch

Cluster (cl)

Keeping last lp of each dc on hook, dc in 3 sts indicated, yo and draw through all 4 lps on hook.

Instructions

Note: *To change color, work until 2 lps of last st rem on hook; with new color, yo and draw through 2 lps on hook. Cut old color.*

With purple, ch 129.

Row 1 (RS): 2 dc in 4th ch from hook (beg 3 skipped chs count as a dc); dc in next 3 chs, [**cl** *(see Pattern Stitch)* over next 3 chs] twice; dc in next 3 chs; *3 dc in each of next 2 chs; dc in next 3 chs, [cl over next 3 chs] twice; dc in next 3 chs; rep from * to last ch; 3 dc in last ch, turn.

Row 2: Ch 3 (counts as a dc on this and following rows), 2 dc in first dc; dc in next 3 sts, [cl over next 3 sts] twice; dc in next 3 sts; *3 dc in each of next 2 sts; dc in next 3 sts, [cl over next 3 sts] twice; dc in next 3 sts; rep from * to beg 3 skipped chs; 3 dc in 3rd ch of beg 3 skipped chs, changing to variegated in last dc, turn. Cut purple.

Row 3: Ch 3, 2 dc in first dc; dc in next 3 sts, cl twice; dc in next 3 sts, *3 dc in each of next 2 sts; dc in next 3 sts, cl twice; dc in next 3 sts; rep from * to turning ch; 3 dc in 3rd ch of turning ch-3, turn.

Row 4: Ch 3, 2 dc in first dc; dc in next 3 sts, cl twice; dc in next 3 sts, *3 dc in each of next 2 sts; dc in next 3 sts, cl twice; dc in next 3 sts; rep from * to turning ch; 3 dc in 3rd ch of turning ch-3, changing to light purple in last dc, turn.

Rows 5 & 6: Rep rows 3 and 4, changing to variegated in last dc.

Rows 7 & 8: Rep rows 3 and 4, changing to yellow in last dc.

Rows 9 & 10: Rep rows 3 and 4, changing to variegated in last dc.

Rows 11 & 12: Rep rows 3 and 4, changing to purple in last dc.

Rows 13 & 14: Rep rows 3 and 4, changing to variegated in last dc.

Rows 15–62: Rep rows 3 through 14 four times more. At end of row 62, do not turn.

Fasten off and weave in all ends.

Tutti Frutti

EASY

Size

About 37 x 50 inches

Materials

Bulky (chunky) weight yarn, 12 oz (370 yds, 180g) white; 6 oz (185 yds, 170g) each red, yellow, blue and green

***Note:** Our photographed afghan was made with Lion Brand Homespun, Hepplewhite #300, covered bridge #367, Sunshine State #372, Montana sky #368 and Florida Keys green #369.*

Size N/15/10mm crochet hook or size needed to obtain gauge

Tapestry needle

Gauge

In pattern, 9 sts = 4 inches

Instructions

***Note:** To change color, work until 2 lps of last st rem on hook; with new color, yo and draw through 2 lps on hook. Cut old color.*

With white, ch 82.

Row 1 (RS): Sc in 2nd ch from hook and in each rem ch, turn.

Row 2: Ch 1, sc in each sc, changing to red in last sc, turn.

Row 3: Ch 1, sc in first 2 sc, hdc in next sc, dc in next 5 sc, hdc in next sc, sc in next sc; ***ch 1, sk next sc, sc in next sc, hdc in next sc, dc in next 5 sc, hdc in next sc, sc in next sc; rep from * to last sc; sc in last sc, turn.

Row 4: Ch 1, sc in first 2 sc, hdc in next hdc, dc in next 5 dc, hdc in next hdc, sc in next sc, ***ch 1, sk next ch-1 sp, sc in next sc, hdc in next hdc, dc in next 5 dc, hdc in next hdc, sc in next sc; rep from * to last sc; sc in last sc, changing to white, turn.

Row 5: Ch 1, sc in each st and ch-1 sp, turn.

Row 6: Ch 1, sc in each sc, changing to yellow in last sc, turn.

Row 7: Ch 2 *(counts as a dc)*, dc in next 2 sc, hdc in next sc, sc in next sc, ch 1, sk next sc, sc in next sc, hdc in next sc; ***dc in next 5 sc, hdc in next sc, sc in next sc, ch 1, sk next sc, sc in next sc, hdc in next sc; rep from * to last 3 sc; dc in last 3 sc, turn.

Row 8: Ch 2, dc in next 2 dc, hdc in next hdc, sc in next sc, ch 1, sc in next sc, hdc in next hdc, ***dc in next 5 dc, hdc in next hdc, sc in next sc, ch 1, sk next ch-1 sp, sc in next sc, hdc in next hdc; rep from * to last 2 dc and turning ch; dc in next 2 dc and in 2nd ch of turning ch-2, changing to white in last dc, turn.

Row 9: Ch 1, sc in each st and ch-1 sp, turn.

Row 10: Ch 1, sc in each sc, changing to blue in last sc, turn.

Rep rows 3 through 10, working in following color sequence until afghan measures about 50 inches, ending with 2 rows white and on RS.

2 rows blue

2 rows white

2 rows green

2 rows white

2 rows red

2 rows white

2 rows yellow

2 rows white

At end of last row, do not change colors.

Edging

Working along next side in ends of rows, sc evenly to row 1. Fasten off.

Hold afghan with RS facing you and unworked long edge at top; join white in end of row 1; ch 1, sc in same row; working in ends of rem rows, sc evenly to last row.

Fasten off and weave all ends.

OUTDOOR
The Ghosts Of Devil's Marsh
M D SPENSER

Shaded Squares

EASY

Size
About 45 x 49 inches

Materials
Medium (worsted) weight yarn, 10 oz (600 yds, 300g) each turquoise, red, orange and blue; 5 oz (300 yds, 150g) each lime, pink, yellow and periwinkle

Size K/10½/6.5mm crochet hook or size needed to obtain gauge

Tapestry needle

Gauge
Square = 7½ inches square

Instructions

Square A (make 11)

With pink, ch 6; join to form a ring.

Rnd 1 (RS): Ch 3 (counts as a dc on this and following rnds), 2 dc in ring; ch 3; ***3** dc in ring; ch 3; rep from ***** twice more; join in 3rd ch of beg ch-3. *(12 dc)*

Rnd 2: Ch 3, dc in next 2 dc, 5 dc in next ch-3 sp, *****dc in next 3 dc, 5 dc in next ch-3 sp; rep from ***** twice more; join in 3rd ch of beg ch-3. *(32 dc)*

Rnd 3: Ch 3, dc in next 4 dc; *****in next dc work (dc, ch 3, dc)—corner made; dc in next 7 dc; rep from ***** twice more; in next dc work (dc, ch 3, dc)—corner made; dc in next 2 dc; join in 3rd ch of beg ch-3. Fasten off.

Rnd 4: Join red in any corner ch-3 sp; ch 3, 4 dc in same sp—beg corner made; *****dc in next 9 dc, 5 dc in next ch-3 sp—corner made; rep from ***** twice more; dc in next 9 dc; join in 3rd ch of beg ch-3.

Rnd 5: Ch 3, dc in next dc; *****in next dc work (dc, ch 3, dc)—corner made; dc in next 13 dc; rep from ***** twice more; in next dc work (dc, ch 3, dc)—corner made; dc in next 11 dc, join in 3rd ch of beg ch-3.

Rnd 6: Ch 3, dc in next 2 dc; ***5** dc in next ch-3 sp—corner made; dc in next 15 dc; rep from ***** twice more; 5 dc in next ch-3 sp—corner made; dc in next 12 dc; join in 3rd ch of beg ch-3.

Fasten off and weave in all ends.

Square B (make 11)

Work same as Square A, working rnds 1 through 3 with periwinkle and rnds 4 through 6 with blue.

Square C (make 10)

Work same as Square A, working rnds 1 through 3 with yellow and rnds 4 through 6 with orange.

Square D (make 10)

Work same as Square A, working rnds 1 through 3 with lime and rnds 4 through 6 with turquoise.

Assembly
Referring to diagram on page 14 for color placement, join squares tog. To join squares, hold 2 squares with right sides tog and carefully match sts. With matching color and leaving 3rd dc of each 5-dc corner unworked, sc in each rem sc across side. Join rem squares in same manner. Weave in all ends.

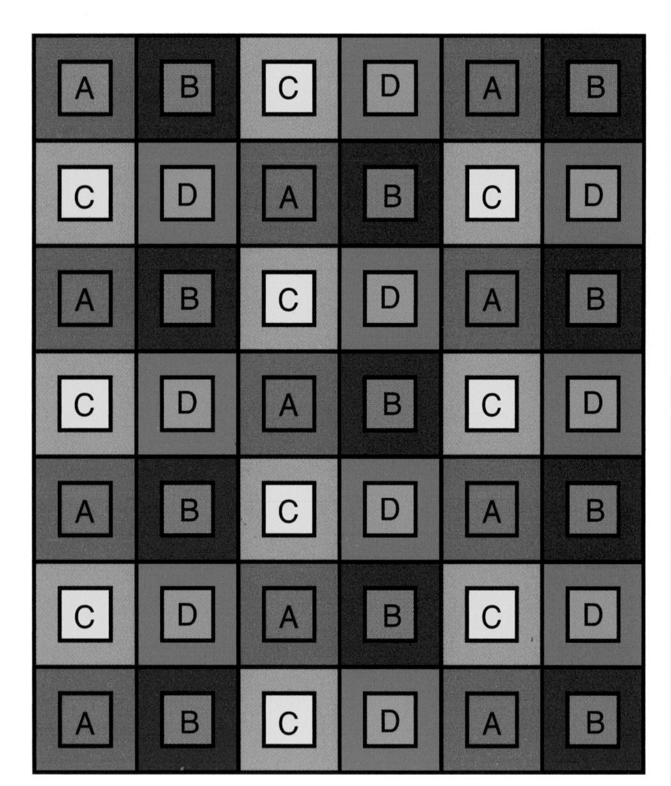

Shaded Squares Afghan

Fringe

Basic Instructions

Cut a piece of cardboard half as long as specified in instructions for strands plus ½" for trimming allowance. Wind yarn loosely and evenly lengthwise around cardboard. When card is filled, cut yarn across one end. Do this several times, then begin fringing; you can wind additional strands as you need them.

Single Knot Fringe

Hold specified number of strands for one knot of fringe together, then fold in half. Hold scarf with right side facing you. Use crochet hook to draw folded end through space or stitch from right to wrong side (**Figs 1** and **2**), pull loose ends through folded section (**Fig 3**) and draw knot up firmly (**Fig 4**). Space knots as indicated in pattern instructions.

Fig 1 **Fig 2** **Fig 3** **Fig 4**

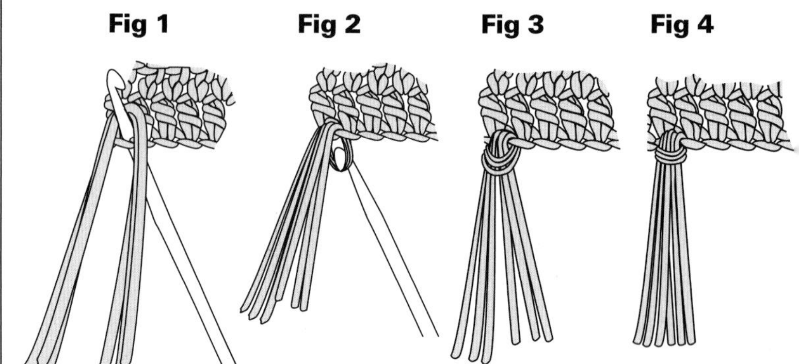

Double Knot Fringe

Begin by working Single Knot Fringe completely across one end of scarf. With right side facing you and working from left to right, take half the strands of one knot and half the strands in the knot next to it, and knot them together (**Fig 5**).

Fig 5

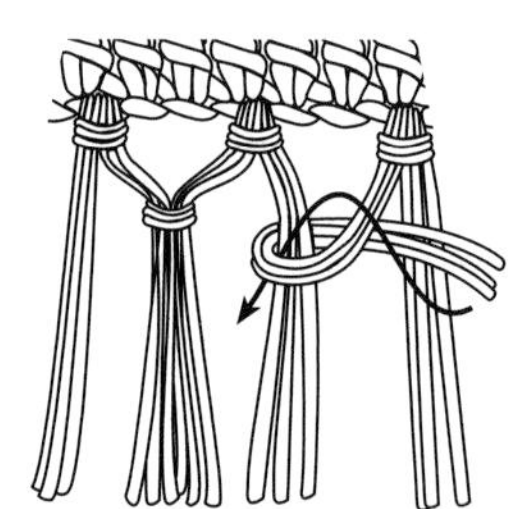

CROCHET HOOKS METRIC CONVERSION CHART

U.S.	1/B	2/C	3/D	4/E	5/F	6/G	8/H	9/I	10/J	10½/K	N
Continental-mm	2.25	2.75	3.25	3.5	3.75	4.25	5	5.5	6	6.5	9.0

How to Check Gauge

A correct stitch gauge is very important. Please take the time to work a stitch gauge swatch about 4 x 4 inches. Measure the swatch. If the number of stitches and rows are fewer than indicated under "Gauge" in the pattern, your hook is too large. Try another swatch with a smaller size hook. If the number of stitches and rows are more than indicated under "Gauge" in the pattern, your hook is too small. Try another swatch with a larger size hook.

Abbreviations & Symbols

beg ... begin/beginning
bpdc ... back post double crochet
bpsc ... back post single crochet
bptr ... back post treble crochet
CC ... contrasting color
ch ... chain stitch
ch- ... refers to chain or space previously made (i.e. ch-1 space)
ch sp ... chain space
cl ... cluster
cm ... centimeter(s)
dc ... double crochet
dc dec ... double crochet 2 or more stitches together, as indicated
dec ... decrease/decreases/decreasing
dtr ... double treble crochet
fpdc ... front post double crochet
fpsc ... front post single crochet
fptr ... front post treble crochet
g ... grams
hdc ... half double crochet
hdc dec ... half double crochet 2 or more stitches together, as indicated
lp(s) ... loops(s)
MC ... main color
mm ... millimeter(s)
oz ... ounce(s)
pc ... popcorn
rem ... remain/remaining
rep ... repeat(s)
rnd(s) ... round(s)
RS ... right side
sc ... single crochet
sc dec ... single crochet 2 or more stitches together, as indicated
sk ... skip
sl st ... slip stitch
sp(s) ... space(s)
st(s) ... stitch(es)
tog ... together
tr ... treble crochet
trtr ... triple treble
WS ... wrong side
yd(s) ... yard(s)
yo ... yarn over

* An asterisk (or double asterisk **) is used to mark the beginning of a portion of instructions to be worked more than once; thus, "rep from * twice more" means after working the instructions once, repeat the instructions following the asterisk twice more (3 times in all).

() Parentheses are used to set off and clarify a group of stitches that are to be worked all into the same space or stitch, such as "in next corner sp work (2 dc, ch 1, 2 dc)."

[] Brackets are used to enclose instructions that should be worked the exact number of times specified immediately following the parentheses, such as "[2 sc in next dc, sc in next dc] twice."

[] Brackets and () parentheses are used to provide additional information to clarify instructions.

Join—join with a sl st unless otherwise specified.

The patterns in this book are written using United States terminology. Terms that have different English equivalents are noted below.

United States	**English**
single crochet (sc)	double crochet (dc)
double crochet (dc)	treble (tr)
treble crochet (tr)	double treble (dtr)
triple treble crochet (trtr)	quadruple treble (q[uad] tr)
skip (sk)	miss
slip stit ch (sl st)	slip stitch (ss) or single crochet
gauge	tension
yarn over (yo)	yarn over hook (YOH)

Skill Levels

BEGINNER
Beginner projects for first-time crocheters using basic stitches. Minimal shaping.

EASY
Easy projects using basic stitches, repetitive stitch patterns, simple color changes and simple shaping and finishing.

INTERMEDIATE
Intermediate projects with a variety of stitches, mid-level shaping and finishing.

EXPERIENCED
Experienced projects using advanced techniques and stitches, detailed shaping and refined finishing.

Stitch Guide

Chain - ch:
YO, draw through lp on hook.

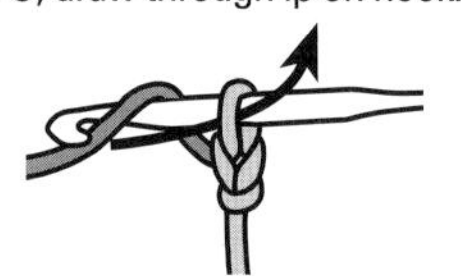

Single Crochet - sc:
Insert hook in st, YO and draw through, YO and draw through both lps on hook.

Reverse Single Crochet - Reverse sc:
Work from left to right, insert hook in sp or st indicated (**a**), draw lp through sp or st - 2 lps on hook (**b**); YO and draw through lps on hook.

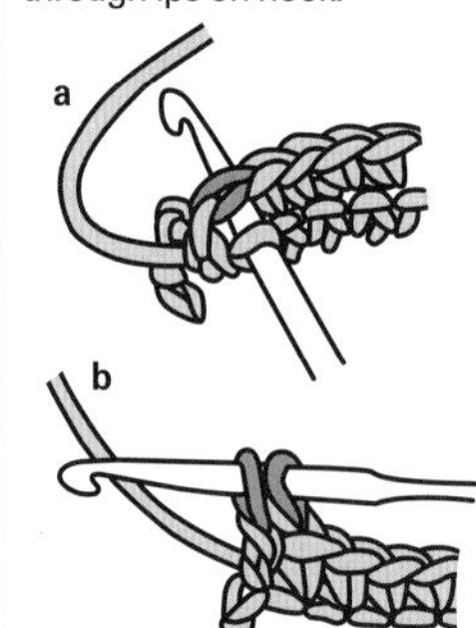

Half Double Crochet - hdc:
YO, insert hook in st, YO, draw through, YO and draw through all 3 lps on hook.

Double Crochet - dc:
YO, insert hook in st, YO, draw through, (YO and draw through 2 lps on hook) twice.

Triple Crochet - trc:
YO twice, insert hook in st, YO, draw through, (YO and draw through 2 lps on hook) 3 times.

Slip Stitch - sl st:
(**a**) **Used for Joinings**
Insert hook in indicated st, YO and draw through st and lp on hook.

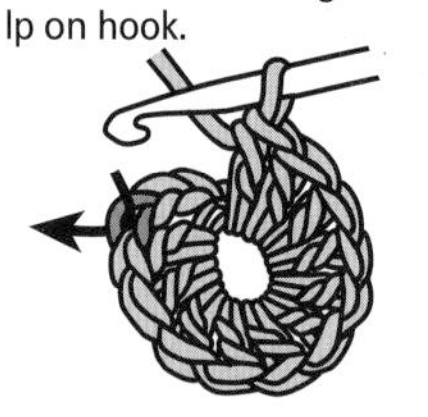

(**b**) **Used for Moving Yarn Over**
Insert hook in st, YO draw through st and lp on hook.

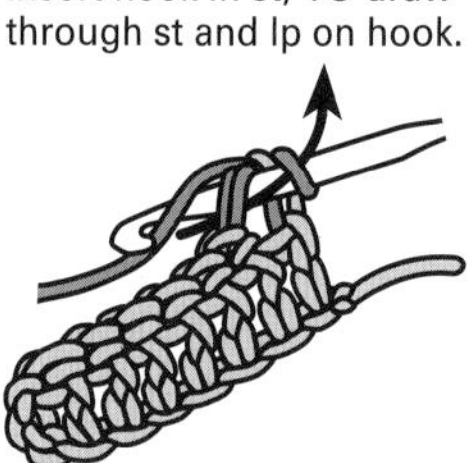

Front Loop - FL:
The front loop is the loop toward you at the top of the stitch.

Back Loop - BL:
The back loop is the loop away from you at the top of the stitch.

Post:
The post is the vertical part of the stitch.

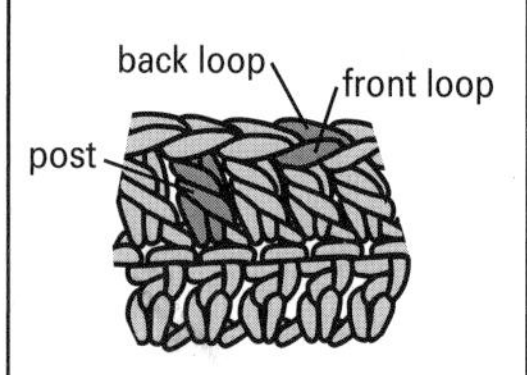

Overcast Stitch is worked loosely to join crochet pieces.

DRG Publishing
306 East Parr Road
Berne, IN 46711

TOLL-FREE ORDER LINE or to request a free catalog (800) 582-6643
Customer Service (800) 282-6643, Fax (800) 882-6643

Visit AnniesAttic.com.

Customer Service (800) 282-6643, **fax** (800) 882-6643

ISBN:1-59012-123-6 Printed in USA 2 3 4 5 6 7 8 9